PITCH TALES

REVEALING THE UNTOLD STORIES OF YOUR BELOVED CRICKETERS

DIVYANSHU GAUR

Copyright © Divyanshu Gaur
All Rights Reserved.

This book has been self-published with all reasonable efforts taken to make the material error-free by the author. No part of this book shall be used, reproduced in any manner whatsoever without written permission from the author, except in the case of brief quotations embodied in critical articles and reviews.

The Author of this book is solely responsible and liable for its content including but not limited to the views, representations, descriptions, statements, information, opinions and references ["Content"]. The Content of this book shall not constitute or be construed or deemed to reflect the opinion or expression of the Publisher or Editor. Neither the Publisher nor Editor endorse or approve the Content of this book or guarantee the reliability, accuracy or completeness of the Content published herein and do not make any representations or warranties of any kind, express or implied, including but not limited to the implied warranties of merchantability, fitness for a particular purpose. The Publisher and Editor shall not be liable whatsoever for any errors, omissions, whether such errors or omissions result from negligence, accident, or any other cause or claims for loss or damages of any kind, including without limitation, indirect or consequential loss or damage arising out of use, inability to use, or about the reliability, accuracy or sufficiency of the information contained in this book.

Made with ♥ on the Notion Press Platform
www.notionpress.com

Dedicated to every soul who has felt the thrill of leather meeting willow, who has savored the scent of freshly cut grass on a cricket field, and who has felt their heart race with anticipation as a match unfolds. To the players who have inspired us with their skill and dedication, and to the fans who have cheered them on through victories and defeats alike, this book is a tribute.

It is dedicated to the early mornings spent perfecting a cover drive, to the afternoons spent debating the nuances of the game with friends, and to the late nights glued to the screen, unable to tear ourselves away from the action. It is a celebration of the love that binds us together as cricket enthusiasts, transcending borders, cultures, and backgrounds.

May these pages serve as a reminder of the joy, camaraderie, and passion that cricket instills in us all. Here's to the countless memories made on the pitch, and to the countless more waiting to be created. This book is for you, the heart and soul of cricket, without whom the game would be nothing but a mere spectacle.

Contents

Foreword   *vii*

Preface   *ix*

Acknowledgements   *xi*

Prologue   *xiii*

1. Masterstroke: Sachin Tendulkars' Tactical Brilliance Against Chris Cairns   1

2. Sehwag And Sachin's Comic Mastery: A Cricketing Showdown With Shoaib Akhtar   4

3. Hangover Heroics: Herschelle Gibbs' Legendary Knock In The Greatest ODI Ever   7

4. Stokes' Heroics: A Triumph Of Grit And Glory   11

5. Controversy At Dambulla: Sehwag's Century Denied By A Deliberate No-Ball   17

6. Yuvraj's Symphony Of Sixes: A Historic Night In Durban   20

7. The Clash On The Field: Harbhajan Singh And Sreesanth's Confrontation   24

8. A Cricketing Nightmare: The Terrorist Attack On The Sri Lankan Team In Pakistan   27

9. The Miracle At Eden Gardens: India's Historic Triumph   31

10. Sachin's Autograph: A Promise Fulfilled   35

11. Resilience Rewritten: Rishabh Pant's Gabba Glory   38

Contents

12. Boundary Drama: The Epic Tale Of The 2019   43
     Cricket World Cup Final

Beyond the Boundary: Wrapping Up and What's   49
Next

Foreword

As I stand on the threshold of these pages, I am reminded of the profound essence that lies within the world of cricket. It is a world where dreams take flight on the wings of ambition, where heroes are born from the crucible of competition, and where stories weave themselves into the fabric of our collective consciousness.

In "Pitch Tales," we are invited to embark on a journey that transcends the boundaries of time and space, delving deep into the heart of cricket to uncover the hidden narratives that have shaped the game we love. Through the eyes of a software developer turned author, we are presented with a fresh perspective, one that blends the precision of code with the passion of a true cricket aficionado.

From the crack of the bat to the roar of the crowd, each page of this book pulsates with the energy of the game, offering us a glimpse into the lives of our favorite cricketers and the untold stories that lie beneath the surface. It is a testament to the enduring power of cricket to captivate and inspire, to unite and transcend, and to remind us of the boundless possibilities that await those who dare to dream.

As you turn the pages of "Pitch Tales," may you be transported to the heart of the action, where every shot is a symphony, every wicket a drama, and every victory a triumph of the human spirit. May you rediscover the magic of cricket in all its glory, and may you be reminded once again of why this game holds such a special place in our hearts.

Foreword by Divyanshu Gaur

Preface

Cricket, with its rich history and timeless allure, has always held a special place in the hearts of millions around the globe. It is a game that transcends boundaries, bringing people together from all walks of life in celebration of skill, camaraderie, and sportsmanship.

In "Pitch Tales," I set out on a journey to explore the unseen facets of cricket, inspired by my passion for the game and fueled by the endless stories that lie beneath its surface. As a software developer turned author, I bring a unique perspective to the table, combining my love for cricket with my expertise in technology to present a fresh take on the sport we all cherish.

This book is not just a collection of anecdotes or statistics; it is a tribute to the spirit of cricket and the countless individuals who have dedicated their lives to its pursuit. Through meticulous research and heartfelt storytelling, I aim to shine a light on the unsung heroes, the behind-the-scenes moments, and the untold tales that have shaped the landscape of cricket over the years.

Whether you're a die-hard fan or a casual observer, I hope that "Pitch Tales" will reignite your passion for the game and inspire you to see cricket in a new light. So, join me as we journey into the heart of the pitch, where every match is a story waiting to be told, and every player is a legend in the making.

Welcome to "Pitch Tales" – where the magic of cricket comes to life on every page.

Divyanshu Gaur

Acknowledgements

Writing "Pitch Tales" has been a labor of love, and I am deeply grateful to all those who have supported me along the way.

From the unwavering support and the guidance of my mentor and the contributions of countless individuals, each has added a unique dimension to this project.

I am grateful for the synchronicities and opportunities provided by the universe, which have aligned to bring this vision to fruition.

Thank you, universe, for the countless ways you have facilitated this journey.

Warm regards, Divyanshu Gaur

Prologue

In the vast arena of cricket, where heroes are immortalized and triumphs celebrated, there exists a parallel narrative often overlooked – one of resilience, camaraderie, and the indomitable human spirit. Welcome to "Pitch Tales," a journey that transcends the boundaries of mere sport to explore the profound depths of the cricketing experience.

As we embark on this journey together, we peel back the layers of time to reveal the forgotten heroes, the pivotal moments, and the dramatic twists that have shaped the game we love. From the dusty fields of village cricket to the grand stages of international competition, we uncover the rich tapestry of cricketing lore that binds us together as fans and players alike.

From the antics of players to the shenanigans of umpires, "Pitch Tales" is your backstage pass to the most hilarious moments cricket has to offer. Get ready to chuckle, guffaw, and maybe even snort with laughter as we delve into the side-splitting stories that make this sport anything but ordinary.

So, grab your cricket bat and your sense of humor, because "Pitch Tales" is about to take you on a riotous romp like no other. It's time to score some belly laughs and hit a six straight into the realm of comedy – all on the hilarious stage of the cricket pitch!

Get set for a side-splitting adventure that will leave you in stitches and have you shouting, "Howzat!" for more.

Divyanshu Gaur

CHAPTER ONE

MASTERSTROKE: SACHIN TENDULKARS' TACTICAL BRILLIANCE AGAINST CHRIS CAIRNS

Former Indian cricketer Sachin Tendulkar shares an interesting story about facing former New Zealand all-rounder Chris Cairns, at a BMW event in Melbourne, Australia when he was interviewed by Max Waller. Tendulkar narrates a story; India was playing against New Zealand in Mohali when Cairns was in the middle of a good bowling spell, bowling at him and Rahul Dravid. Tendulkar reveals that the ball was reverse-swinging and Cairns was beating them two to three times in the over. Tendulkar mentions that they were getting beaten as they were clueless as to where the shine was and where the rough

side was on the ball. An idea struck Tendulkar which he discussed with Dravid. He told Dravid

that from the non-striker's end since he was closer to the bowler Cairns, he could observe when the bowler would take up his mark which side is shinny and which is rough. So, what he would do is – if Cairns gripped the ball to bowl an out-swinger then Tendulkar would hold the bat in his left hand, and if

Cairns was to bowl an in-swinger then Tendulkar would hold the bat with his right hand at the non-striker's end.

Cricket greets Sachin Tendulkar and Chris Cairns in the heat of competition

The whole audience had a laugh when Tendulkar revealed this. Humorously, he narrates that it was the only time in his career that he saw a batsman taking guard watched the non-striker, instead of watching the wrist of

the bowler. The idea worked and runs flowed from the bat of Dravid and Tendulkar. While Tendulkar was doing this, the New Zealand fielders figured out what the Indian batsmen were up to as normally a non-striker would not look back at the bowler when he was at his crease. It was Cairns' time to answer back and he bowled a cross-seamed delivery, after which he looked at Tendulkar and said, "What
have you got for this?"

Sachin and Dravid's out-of-the-box strategy that helped them overcome Chris Cairns is pure gold

The Indian batting maestro was however a 'step ahead'. He concluded that he had warned Dravid that if he did not know what was coming, he would hold the bat in the middle. His response led to applause and laughter among the audience.

CHAPTER TWO

Sehwag and Sachin's Comic Mastery: A Cricketing Showdown with Shoaib Akhtar

In a high-stakes match against Pakistan, the stage was set for a showdown between two cricketing giants: Shoaib Akhtar and Virender Sehwag. Shoaib, known for his lightning-fast deliveries, found himself in a tight spot against Sehwag's aggressive batting.

Running out of options, Shoaib decided to resort to intimidation tactics. With a bag of bouncers and a plan to ruffle Sehwag's feathers, he charged in from around the wicket, aiming to unsettle the Indian opener.

After each thunderous delivery, Shoaib, with a smirk on his face, taunted Sehwag, challenging him to take on the bouncer barrage.

Shoaib: "Hook maar ke dikha." ("Hit me with your best hook shot")

Sehwag, however, remained unfazed by Shoaib's attempts to distract him. With a characteristic grin, he fired back:

Sehwag: "Yeh bowling kar raha hai ya bheekh maang raha hai?"

His response not only silenced Shoaib but also elicited chuckles from both teams.

Realizing that Shoaib was committed to his strategy, Sehwag decided to turn the tables. Walking up to Shoaib, he dropped a bombshell:

Sehwag: "Wo tera baap khada hai non-striker end pe, usko bol woh marke dikhayega."

Little did Shoaib know that the "baap" at the non-striker's end was none other than the legendary Sachin Tendulkar.

As fate would have it, Shoaib unleashed a similar bouncer to Sachin, expecting a different result. But Sachin, the master of timing and precision, effortlessly dispatched the ball over the ropes for a colossal six.

In the aftermath, Sehwag delivered the final blow to Shoaib's ego with his now-iconic line:

Sehwag: "Baap baap hota hai, beta beta hota hai." (Dads rule, kids drool)

Witnessing Sachin's sixer response to Akhtar, pure joy
etched on his face

Laughter echoed across the field as Sehwag's words sank
in, showcasing not only Sehwag and Sachin's cricketing
prowess but also their ability to turn pressure situations
into moments of levity, leaving the cricketing world in awe
of their brilliance both on and off the field.

Hangover Heroics: Herschelle Gibbs' Legendary Knock in the Greatest ODI Ever

In the annals of cricket history, one date stands out as a testament to the sheer drama and brilliance of the game: December 12, 2006. It was a day when records were shattered, legends were made, and Herschelle Gibbs etched his name in cricketing folklore.

On that fateful day, South Africa and Australia clashed in the fifth ODI at the Wanderers, Johannesburg. Little did the world know that they were about to witness a match that would go down as the greatest ever in 50-over cricket.

Australia, batting first, unleashed their formidable batting lineup, led by the indomitable Ricky Ponting. With a masterful 164-run innings, Ponting propelled the Aussies to an imposing total of 434 runs, setting the stage for an epic showdown.

But it was during South Africa's chase that the true heroics unfolded, courtesy of Herschelle Gibbs. However, what made his innings even more remarkable was the revelation that he was nursing a hangover from a night of revelry just hours before the match.

In his autobiography, 'To the Point: The No-holds Barred Autobiography', Gibbs candidly admitted to his less-than-ideal preparation for the monumental clash. Despite battling the effects of a late-night drinking session that stretched until 1 AM, Gibbs stepped onto the field determined to make an impact. And make an impact he did.

With sheer determination and an unparalleled display of skill, Gibbs unleashed a barrage of boundaries and towering sixes, dismantling the Australian bowling attack with disdain. His career-best knock of 175 runs, adorned with 21 fours and 7 sixes, not only defied the odds but also propelled South Africa towards an improbable victory.

As Gibbs blazed his way to glory, the Wanderers erupted in disbelief and awe. The hangover that threatened to derail his performance became a mere footnote in the face of his monumental achievement.

South Africa's chase of 434 runs not only secured a historic win but also etched itself into the annals of cricketing history as the highest successful run chase in ODI cricket.

Gibbs' epic 175: A moment of triumph amidst the high-stakes clash against Australia in the historic 434 chase

The match, hailed as the greatest ever 50-over encounter, showcased the resilience, skill, and sheer audacity of Herschelle Gibbs, forever cementing his place among cricket's immortals

CHAPTER FOUR

Stokes' Heroics: A Triumph of Grit and Glory

A day that began full of possibility flipped and flopped and flipped again on the balance of probablility and ended with an air of impossibility as England kept the Ashes alive, thanks to Stokes' match-winning century. His unbeaten 135 handed England the most unlikely of victories, by one wicket, in the third Test at Headingley, allowing them to level the series at 1-1.

In one of the most thrilling finishes imaginable - well, since England's World Cup triumph last month with, you guessed it, Stokes, front and centre - he and Jack Leach stood up against the odds and steered their side to their highest successful run chase in Tests, two days after they had been humbled for 67 in their first innings and were then set 359 to win.

The pivotal drop of Stokes at 116 during the
Headingley Test

Numerous times Australia threatened to take the final wicket they needed for a victory that had seemed inevitable, only to fluff their lines repeatedly.

Stokes was dropped on 116 when he sent a top edge off Pat Cummins towards third man, where Marcus Harris got his hands to it but couldn't hold on. Australia then wasted a review - which would come back to haunt them - when Cummins rapped Leach on the pad and the DRS confirmed the ball had pitched well outside leg.

When Stokes just cleared the man on the rope for a six off Nathan Lyon, the crowd went wild and England needed just two more to win. Two balls later, Leach should have been run out after going for a non-existent single, but Lyon fumbled as he tried to gather the throw from backward point. Stokes should have been out lbw attempting to slog-sweep the very next ball, which was pitching on middle and leg and shown by Hawk-Eye to be hitting the stumps, but with no reviews left, Australia could do nothing.

The hosts had dared to dream when they resumed on a hot summer's day at 156 for 3 with Joe Root unbeaten on 75 and Stokes locked and loaded having faced 50 balls for his 2 not out.

Cue the possibility. These two batsmen at the crease - Root with a point to ram home after going some way to answering critics of his batting, captaincy and combination of both, and Stokes with a fifty and a Man-of-the-Match century to his name in the previous two Tests - were fully capable of bringing England within reach of the 203 runs still needed to clinch victory.

Turning the tide with a towering shot during the
Headingley Test showdown

Cue the probability. Australia's attack, while frustrated on the third afternoon, had kept the pressure on and, with the second new ball due after eight overs on day four, England faced a big task just to navigate the morning, let alone chase down the target. That became even more unlikely when Root fell, having added just two runs, to a brilliant slip catch from David Warner - his sixth of the match - off the bowling of Lyon in the sixth over of the day.

Stokes and Jonny Bairstow swung the probability back in England's favour with a defiant, and threatening, 86-run partnership. Their union was broken when Bairstow, on 36, attempted to cut Josh Hazlewood but guided the ball to Marnus Labuschagne at second slip.

Cue the impossibility. Stokes' knock, which included 11 fours and eight sixes, also saw him farm the strike expertly, while England No. 11 Leach deserved huge plaudits for holding his nerve in a 76-run partnership with Stokes off 62 balls, to which Leach contributed 1 off 17. Only once in the history of Test cricket - actually only a few months ago, in Durban - has a last-wicket pair scored more to secure victory.

Stokes had looked like running out of partners. Jos Buttler, initially called through and then sent back by Stokes, was run out to a direct hit from Travis Head, Chris Woakes chipped Hazlewood straight to Matthew Wade at a short extra cover, Jofra Archer holed out after a brief cameo and Stuart Broad was out lbw to a James Pattinson yorker.

A breathtaking display as Stokes nears victory single-handedly against every bowler

As Stokes neared his century, Hazlewood - who was one wicket away from claiming 10 for the match - returned to the attack. Stokes proceeded to take 19 off the over, bringing up his ton with a four hammered through wide long-on, and following up with consecutive sixes.

Stokes admitted there were moments when he wasn't part of the action that he couldn't watch. Leach levelled the scores with a single off Cummins and when Stokes brought up the win on the next ball, flaying Cummins through the covers to the boundary, he let out an almighty roar, arms outstretched as Leach ran to embrace him like the saviour he was.

Stokes' triumphant roar echoes across the field as he clinches victory with a decisive run

It seemed like so long ago that Stokes had toiled with the ball for 24.2 overs to claim 3 for 56 in Australia's second innings when Labuschagne top-scored for the tourists for the third time in as many innings with 80. It made Stokes' feats with the bat all the more remarkable.

CONTROVERSY AT DAMBULLA: SEHWAG'S CENTURY DENIED BY A DELIBERATE NO-BALL

The incident took place during the third ODI of the Sri Lanka tri-series (also featuring New Zealand) clash between India and Sri Lanka at Dambulla in 2010. The India spinners had bowled out Sri Lanka for 170, and India closed in on the target after Sehwag's one-man blitzkrieg. At the beginning of the 35th over, India needed five runs to win, and Sehwag needed merely one run to complete his century.

Randiv's first ball kept very low, beating both the batter and keeper Kumar Sangakkara. The result was four byes.

Sehwag failed to put away the next two deliveries but went down the track off the fourth ball. He hit it for a six, raising his arms in celebration for what would have been his hundred and the winning run.

Unbeknownst to the opener, the umpire had already signaled a front-foot no-ball, accounting for the winning run and leaving Sehwag stranded on 99.

Suraj Randiv's questionable delivery denies Sehwag a century, sparking debate over fair play

There was widespread speculation that this was deliberate, with reports floating around, including one that said Sri Lanka skipper Kumar Sangakkara could be allegedly heard on the stump mic saying in Sinhalese "If he hits the ball, he gets the run": which could easily have been an innocuous statement in itself.

What made matters worse was that the no-ball was quite big. In the post-match conference, Kumar Sangakkara stated: "If it is deliberate and I don't think he is that sort of player. But if it is deliberate of course I need to have a chat with him and make sure that things like that don't happen again. I also need to see whether there was any talk on the field before that delivery."

He did say that his feeling was that the no-ball was deliberate: "But knowing Suraj, he is a nice guy, I do not doubt that it was not intentional... I don't think it is deliberate at all."

Initially, Sehwag said, "I think bowlers try to bowl a wide or no-ball when a batsman is on 99, and scores get level in cricket. It happens in cricket because no one wants a batsman to score a hundred against them. So it's fair enough."

But later on, he targeted Randiv and the Sri Lanka team in the post-match conference.

"He didn't bowl a single no-ball in the Test series or the One-day series so far, so why now on 99? Also, it was not a small no-ball, no margin at all." He continued, "I'm not the captain or player of the opposition team, that I can tell if someone told Randiv to bowl the no-ball or not. But something must've been said. They did the same against Sachin Tendulkar in Cuttack."

In the aftermath, Randiv was handed a one-match ban, while Tillakaratne Dilshan was also fined for encouraging the youngster to bowl a no-ball. Sangakkara was advised by the board to ensure such incidents were not repeated in the future.

CHAPTER SIX

Yuvraj's Symphony of Sixes: A Historic Night in Durban

It was September 19, 2007, a day that would be forever etched in the annals of cricket history. The stage was set at Kingsmead, Durban, as India faced off against England in the inaugural T20 World Cup. The match was poised on a knife's edge, and little did the spectators know, they were about to witness a spectacle like never before.

As Yuvraj Singh walked out to bat, the tension in the air was palpable. England's Stuart Broad was the bowler, and with Andrew Flintoff lurking nearby, the atmosphere crackled with intensity. There was a brief exchange of words between Yuvraj and Flintoff, a glimpse of the fiery competitiveness that was to come. But Yuvraj remained unfazed, his focus solely on the task at hand.

Yuvraj Singh and Flintoff exchange heated words,
setting the stage for cricketing history

As Broad began his run-up, the crowd held its breath. The first ball was pitched up, and Yuvraj wasted no time in dispatching it into the stands with a thunderous swing of his bat.

1. *First Six*: Ravi Shastri's voice boomed over the stadium speakers, "Yuvraj Singh, you beauty! Into the stands, it goes! That's gone miles, way into the crowd! What a way to start!"

The second ball was met with the same fate, soaring high into the Durban sky.

2. *Second Six*: "Oh, he's done it again! Yuvraj Singh is on fire! That's another maximum! He's taking Stuart Broad to the cleaners!" exclaimed Shastri, his excitement infectious.

The third delivery disappeared over long off, leaving the fielders mere spectators.

3. *Third Six*: "It's raining sixes at the Kingsmead! Yuvraj Singh is in a league of his own! That's outta here!"

roared Shastri, as the crowd erupted in cheers.

The fourth ball was sent packing over midwicket, as Yuvraj showcased his sublime timing and power.

Six balls, six sixes, one unforgettable display of cricketing brilliance captured in a single frame

4. *Fourth Six*: "Unbelievable! Yuvraj Singh is making a mockery of this bowling attack! That's disappearing quicker than you can blink!" exclaimed Shastri, barely able to keep up with the action.

With each successive six, the crowd's roar grew louder, the atmosphere reaching fever pitch. As the fifth ball sailed over deep square leg,

5. *Fifth Six*: Shastri's voice echoed across the stadium, "And another one! Yuvraj Singh is unstoppable! The crowd is going wild! This is cricket at its absolute best!"

And then came the moment that would be etched in cricketing folklore forever. As Broad prepared to deliver the sixth ball, the tension was palpable. The stadium fell silent, holding its breath.

6. *Sixth Six*: Yuvraj you beauty, es, six sixes in an over, into the crowd, Yuvraj Singh finishes things off in style sending the ball soaring into the stands for the sixth consecutive time, the eruption was deafening.

"History! Yuvraj Singh has etched his name in the record books! Six sixes in an over! What a moment! Take a bow, Yuvraj Singh!" bellowed Shastri, his voice a mix of awe and reverence.

Stuart Broad's disbelief echoes through his expression after witnessing Yuvraj Singh's unprecedented six sixes onslaught

As Yuvraj raised his bat in triumph, the crowd rose to its feet, applauding the maestro who had just orchestrated a symphony of sixes. It was a moment that transcended the boundaries of the sport, a moment that would be remembered for generations to come. Yuvraj Singh had conquered the sixes, leaving an indelible mark on the game of cricket.

CHAPTER SEVEN

The Clash on the Field: Harbhajan Singh and Sreesanth's Confrontation

In April 2008, during the inaugural season of the Indian Premier League (IPL), a heated altercation between two Indian cricketers, Harbhajan Singh and Sreesanth, shocked the cricketing world and created ripples of controversy.

The incident occurred after a match between the Mumbai Indians, led by Harbhajan Singh, and the Kings XI Punjab, where Sreesanth was representing. It was a tense encounter on the field, with both teams fiercely competing for victory.

During the post-match handshake, Sreesanth, known for his animated demeanor, approached Harbhajan with an outstretched hand. However, what followed took everyone by surprise. Harbhajan, visibly agitated by something, suddenly slapped Sreesanth across the face.

The reason behind Harbhajan's action was speculated to be a result of Sreesanth's behavior during the match. Sreesanth was known for his on-field antics, often engaging in verbal spats and aggressive gestures, which might have irked Harbhajan.

Sreesanth's tearful reaction following the controversial on-field incident involving a slap from Harbhajan Singh

After the incident, chaos ensued on the field, with players and officials rushing to intervene and calm the situation. Harbhajan was immediately reprimanded by the match officials and faced severe backlash from fans and cricketing authorities.

The IPL governing council took swift action, imposing a ban on Harbhajan Singh for the remainder of the IPL season. Additionally, Harbhajan was fined a substantial amount for his conduct, reflecting the severity of the incident.

Both Harbhajan Singh and Sreesanth issued public apologies following the altercation, expressing regret for their actions and emphasizing the importance of sportsmanship and mutual respect on the field.

Despite the controversy, the incident served as a reminder of the passion and intensity that often accompany professional sports. It also highlighted the need for players to maintain composure and uphold the spirit of the game, even in the face of heated competition.

From conflict to camaraderie: Harbhajan and Sreesanth mend fences

In the aftermath of the incident, both Harbhajan Singh and Sreesanth learned valuable lessons about sportsmanship and professionalism, and their altercation remains a cautionary tale in the annals of cricket history.

CHAPTER EIGHT

A Cricketing Nightmare: The Terrorist Attack on the Sri Lankan Team in Pakistan

It was a crisp morning on March 3, 2009, when the Sri Lankan cricket team bus rolled into the Gaddafi Stadium in Lahore, Pakistan. The players were gearing up for the third day of the second Test match against Pakistan, unaware that they were about to face one of the darkest days in cricketing history.

As the team bus approached the stadium, gunmen armed with rifles and grenades ambushed the convoy. The attackers unleashed a barrage of gunfire, targeting the bus carrying the Sri Lankan players and their support staff. Chaos erupted as bullets rained down on the bus, shattering windows and puncturing the metal exterior.

Amidst the panic and confusion, several Sri Lankan players sustained injuries in the attack. Among them were Thilan Samaraweera, who was hit in the leg, and Ajantha Mendis, who suffered shrapnel wounds. The team's assistant coach, Paul Farbrace, was also injured in the gunfire.

Sri Lankan cricket team targeted in terror attack during Pakistan tour, player injured in the harrowing assault

In the face of imminent danger, the Sri Lankan players showed remarkable courage and composure. Despite their injuries, they remained resilient and focused on ensuring the safety of everyone on board. With bullets flying around them, the players helped shield each other from harm and provided support to the injured.

Amidst the chaos, the quick thinking of the team's bus driver played a crucial role in averting further tragedy. Sensing the danger, he maneuvered the bus skillfully, navigating through the narrow streets of Lahore to safety. His actions saved the lives of the Sri Lankan players and prevented a potential massacre.

As news of the attack spread, the cricketing world was left in shock and disbelief. The incident sent shockwaves through the sporting community, raising serious concerns about the safety and security of international cricket in Pakistan.

In the aftermath of the attack, the Sri Lankan cricket team was evacuated from Pakistan under heavy security. Several players sustained injuries and were treated for their wounds upon returning home. The attack prompted widespread condemnation from cricketing authorities and led to Pakistan being stripped of its hosting rights for international cricket tournaments.

Helicopter lands on the ground to swiftly evacuate injured Sri Lankan player after the tragic terror attack during the Pakistan tour

Despite the harrowing ordeal they endured, the courage and resilience displayed by the Sri Lankan players in the face of adversity served as a testament to the unbreakable spirit of cricket. Their actions on that fateful day will be remembered as a shining example of bravery in the face of terror.

The Miracle at Eden Gardens: India's Historic Triumph

It was March 11, 2001, and the cricketing world was abuzz with anticipation as the second Test between India and Australia commenced at Eden Gardens in Kolkata. The Australian team, riding high on a record-breaking winning streak of 16 consecutive Tests, were considered invincible, while India found themselves reeling from a demoralizing defeat in the previous Test at Wankhede Stadium in Mumbai.

From the outset, Australia asserted their dominance, with skipper Steve Waugh winning the toss and electing to bat first. Openers Michael Slater and Matthew Hayden laid a solid foundation, stitching together a century partnership and putting the Indian bowlers under immense pressure. However, a dramatic collapse ensued, triggered by the spin wizardry of Harbhajan Singh, who wreaked havoc with his mesmerizing deliveries. Harbhajan's magical spell culminated in the first-ever Test hat-trick by an Indian bowler, leaving Australia reeling at 269/8 by the end of Day 1.

Day 2 dawned with Australia's hopes resting on the experienced shoulders of Steve Waugh. The Australian captain led from the front, displaying grit and determination as he notched up a magnificent century, crossing numerous milestones along the way. With able support from Jason Gillespie and Glenn McGrath, Waugh propelled Australia to a formidable total of 445, defying the Indian bowlers and raising hopes of another dominant victory.

Laxman and Dravid's masterclass in the historic 2001 Kolkata Test reshapes cricketing destiny

India's response in the first innings faltered, with the top-order crumbling under pressure. However, amidst the ruins emerged VVS Laxman, showcasing sublime strokeplay and resilience as he anchored the innings with a fluent fifty. Despite Laxman's heroics, India found themselves staring down the barrel, trailing by a mammoth margin of 274 runs.

As India took to the crease for the second innings, the odds seemed insurmountable. Yet, amidst the gloom, a ray of hope emerged in the form of Laxman and Rahul Dravid. The duo embarked on a monumental partnership, defying the Australian attack with their unwavering resolve and exquisite batting prowess. Day 3 witnessed a dramatic turnaround, as Laxman's majestic double century and Dravid's gritty century propelled India to a commanding position, setting the stage for a historic comeback.

On Day 4, Laxman and Dravid continued their sublime form, scripting a tale of resilience and determination as they batted throughout the day without being dismissed. Their monumental partnership of 376 runs not only turned the tide in India's favor but also etched their names in cricketing folklore.

Harbhajan singh six-wicket haul in the kolkata Test sets India on course for a memorable win

With a target of 384 set for Australia on the final day, the stage was set for a thrilling climax. Despite a strong start from the Australian openers, Harbhajan Singh and Sachin Tendulkar orchestrated a stunning collapse, dismantling the Australian batting lineup with their spin wizardry. Harbhajan's heroics, coupled with Tendulkar's crucial breakthroughs, sealed India's remarkable victory by 171 runs, marking only the third instance of a team winning after following on in Test cricket history.

Jubilant celebrations mark a famous victory

As the Eden Gardens erupted in jubilation, India basked in the glory of an unforgettable triumph, epitomizing the spirit of resilience and a never-say-die attitude. The Miracle at Eden Gardens will forever be etched in the annals of cricketing history as a testament to the indomitable spirit of the Indian cricket team.

CHAPTER TEN

Sachin's Autograph: A Promise Fulfilled

In the vast tapestry of cricketing legends, few tales shine as brightly as that of Sachin Tendulkar, the Master Blaster whose exploits on the field are matched only by his humility off it. Among the myriad stories that adorn his illustrious career, one stands out as a testament to his unparalleled skill and unwavering determination.

It was October 5, 2007, a day etched in the memory of cricket fans around the world. The third ODI between India and Australia was underway in Hyderabad, with Team India chasing a formidable target of 291 runs. Sachin Tendulkar, accompanied by Gautam Gambhir, took to the crease with the weight of expectations resting squarely on their shoulders.

In the 20th over of the match, Australian spinner Brad Hogg delivered a wicked delivery that bamboozled even the great Tendulkar, sending his stumps cartwheeling. Despite Yuvraj Singh's heroic century, Team India fell short, succumbing to defeat by 47 runs.

Sachin Tendulkar dismissed by Brad Hogg, who
celebrates the key wicket

But it wasn't the match result that would be remembered most vividly from that day; it was a seemingly innocuous moment off the field that would go on to define the course of cricketing history.

After the match, as players exchanged pleasantries and signed autographs for fans, Brad Hogg, the man who had dismissed Tendulkar, approached the Indian maestro with a request for an autograph. Little did he know that this simple act would set in motion a chain of events that would leave an indelible mark on the cricketing world.

In an interview with The Sunday Age, Hogg revealed that Sachin Tendulkar had graciously obliged, signing a photograph for him. But it was the message accompanying the autograph that would leave Hogg both bemused and intrigued: "It won't happen again - Sachin."

At first, Hogg dismissed the message as mere banter, a playful jest from one competitor to another. But Sachin Tendulkar, true to his word, was deadly serious. And so began a remarkable saga of determination and dominance that would see Tendulkar thwart Hogg's every attempt to dismiss him on the cricket field.

Despite facing off against each other 17 times after that fateful match, Hogg never again tasted success against Tendulkar. For the Indian maestro, it was a promise made and a promise kept, a testament to his unparalleled skill and unyielding resolve.

In the end, it wasn't just about a cricketing rivalry; it was about mutual respect and admiration between two titans of the game. And as Sachin Tendulkar continued to weave his magic on the field, leaving bowlers in his wake, Brad Hogg could only marvel at the honor of sharing the pitch with a legend like him

RESILIENCE REWRITTEN: RISHABH PANT'S GABBA GLORY

In the cauldron of the Gabba, where legends are forged and dreams shattered, unfolded a saga of courage, resilience, and unyielding spirit - the Gabba Test of January 2021.

Australia, the reigning champions, had set a daunting target of 328 runs for victory, leaving India with a mountain to climb on the final day of the test match. As the sun beat down relentlessly, the Indian team took to the field, their resolve tested to the limits against a relentless Australian attack.

Cheteshwar Pujara and Ravichandran Ashwin, the linchpins of India's batting lineup, found themselves at the forefront of a brutal assault from the Australian bowlers. Each delivery seemed to carry the weight of Australia's expectations, aimed at breaking the spirit of the Indian duo.

Pujara, enduring the body blows, stands tall as the
unyielding wall in the Gabba Test of 2021

But Pujara, the rock of India's batting order, stood firm
amidst the storm, his defense unyielding, his determination
unwavering. Alongside him, Ashwin, with his astute
judgment and solid technique, weathered the barrage of
bouncers and yorkers, inching India closer to the
improbable target.

However, as the day wore on and the required runs
seemed to drift further away, frustration began to creep
in. The Australian bowlers, sensing victory within their
grasp, unleashed a relentless assault, testing the mettle of
the Indian batsmen with every delivery.

Rishabh Pant's explosive innings takes charge against the Aussie bowlers, showcasing his aggressive batting prowess with a towering six

As the scoreboard ticked over, the tension reached a fever pitch. With wickets falling around them and the target seeming increasingly distant, hope seemed to fade with each passing moment.

But just when all seemed lost, a glimmer of hope emerged from the depths of despair. Rishabh Pant, the enigmatic wicketkeeper-batsman known for his audacious stroke play and fearless approach, strode to the crease with a steely determination in his eyes.

At that moment, India's required runs stood at a daunting 183, with the match hanging in the balance and the hopes of a nation resting on Pant's broad shoulders.

With the crowd holding its breath and the Gabba pulsating with tension, Pant unleashed a breathtaking assault on the Australian bowlers, his bat a blur of motion as he dispatched deliveries to all corners of the ground.

Rishabh Pant seals the historic victory with a decisive winning run at the Gabba, conquering the Australian fortress

With Pujara and Ashwin providing a solid foundation at one end, Pant launched a blistering counterattack, taking the fight to the Australians with an array of breathtaking strokes.

As the runs flowed freely and the target rapidly dwindled, the momentum shifted decisively in India's favor. Pant, with his fearless batting, had breathed new life into India's faltering chase, inspiring his teammates and capturing the imagination of cricket fans around the world.

Indian camp erupts in jubilation as Rishabh Pant savors the sweet taste of victory after conquering the Gabba fortress

And when the final runs were scored and the Gabba erupted in jubilation, it was not just a victory for India, but a triumph of the human spirit. and the famous line Vivek Rajdan said 'tuta hai gabba ka ghamand, jeet gya hai Bharat' , which means India broke Australia fort. In the heart of Brisbane, amidst the echoing chants of passionate cricket fans, Rishabh Pant had etched his name into the annals of cricketing history, his heroics a testament to the power of belief, determination, and unwavering resolve.

CHAPTER TWELVE

BOUNDARY DRAMA: THE EPIC TALE OF THE 2019 CRICKET WORLD CUP FINAL

Many disputed matches have been seen in cricket history but rarely seen as World Cup 2019 final (World Cup 2019 Final). Today, 2 years ago, England captured the World Cup 2019 and defeated New Zealand (England vs New Zealand) in the final. In this match, New Zealand neither lost nor wicket, but still became world champion England. On 14 July 2019, England became the world champion based on the boundary. This disputed rule of the ICC broke the hearts of New Zealand and its fans and England captured the ODI World Cup for the first time. How broken the heart of Kievis and how England became the world champion. Know what was the story of World Cup 2019.

Captains Williamson and Morgan pose with the trophy
before the 2019 Cricket World Cup finals

In the World Cup final, New Zealand captain Ken
Williamson chose to bat first to win the toss. New Zealand
scored 241 for 8 wickets in 50 overs, with Henry Nichols'
half-century and Tom Latham's 47 runs. In response,
England lost their 4 wickets at 86 runs, but after that, Ben
Stokes and Jose Butler crossed the best innings game team
by 200. When England were on the threshold of victory,
Fergusson and Jimmy Neesham bowled well and gave the
hosts a shock. Fergusson broke the partnership by
dismissing Jose Butler for 59, and after that, he also
managed to take the wicket of Chris Woakes. Neesham
dismissed Liam Plunkett and Joffra Archer to make the
match exciting.

The thrill of the final over

England had a 15-run concierge in the final over of the
match. Stokes was on strike and Trent Bolt was bowling
in front of him. Bolt did not give a single run on the first
two balls but Stokes hit a six on the midwicket on the

third ball. After this, what happened on the fourth ball broke the heart of the New Zealand fans. Stokes played the shot at midwicket on the fourth ball. Stokes ran for two runs and Martin Gaptil, standing at midwicket, threw a throw towards the wicketkeeper. But during this time the ball hit the bat of Stokes and went to the boundary line. The umpire gave England 6 runs and the result was now England only needed 3 runs on the last two balls.

Stokes gestures innocence after an accidental deflection results in a boundary, signaling it's not his mistake

On the fifth ball of the bold, Stokes once again tried to take two runs but Adil Rashid was run out in the second run. The same thing happened on the last ball and Mark Wood was run out in a round of two runs. In this way, the World Cup final tie was done and the fight went to the super over.

Super over drama

Super Over also saw a drama that fans would never have thought of. While Butler and Stokes landed at the crease from England in the super over, the Kiwi captain once again bowled the bolt. Stokes scored three runs on the first ball and Butler could score the same run on the second ball. After this, Stokes took a four off England to 8 runs at midwicket. Butler hit the final ball and scored England for 15 runs.

Buttler's lightning-quick run-out seals the victory for England in the thrilling Super Over

Jimmy Neesham and Martin Gaptil went on to bat for New Zealand. In front of him was fast bowler Jofra Archer. Archer threw the first ball wide and Nisham scored two runs on the second ball. After this, Nisham brought a six-root New Zealand to the match on Archer's second ball. Neesham then scored 3 runs on the third ball and now New

Zealand needed 5 runs on the last two balls. Archer scored 3 runs on the next two balls and New Zealand had two runs on the final ball. Martin Gaptil was on strike but on the final ball, Gaptil was run out for two runs and the super over was also tied. But according to ICC rules, the England team with more boundaries was declared the world champion. New Zealand had accumulated 2 sixes, and 14 fours in the match and England had 2 sixes and 22 fours. In this way, England won the World Cup for the first time on the basis of the boundary rule.

Stokes shines as Man of the Match, while teammates thank the crowd, celebrating a memorable victory

In the aftermath of the intense final, both teams showcased remarkable sportsmanship and camaraderie. Despite the heartbreak of defeat, the New Zealand team earned widespread admiration for their grace in accepting the outcome. They displayed humility and resilience, exemplifying the true spirit of the game. Meanwhile, England's victory marked a historic moment, igniting celebrations across the nation and cementing their status as cricketing champions. The final not only etched itself into the annals of cricket history but also served as a testament to the thrilling unpredictability and enduring allure of the sport.

Beyond The Boundary: Wrapping Up And What's Next

Dear Reader,

As we reach the end of our cricketing journey, it's time to reflect on the innings we've shared in "Pitch Tales." In this closing chapter, we take a moment to pause and savor the memories, the laughter, and the camaraderie that have made this book so special.

From the highs of victory to the lows of defeat, from the hilarious mishaps to the heartwarming triumphs, each story has left an indelible mark on our cricketing souls. We've traveled the globe, from the sun-soaked pitches of Australia to the bustling streets of India, exploring the rich tapestry of cricket's global appeal.

But "Pitch Tales" is more than just a collection of cricketing anecdotes – it's a celebration of the spirit of the game, the bonds of friendship, and the joy of storytelling. It's a testament to the enduring power of cricket to unite us across cultures, generations, and backgrounds.

As we bid farewell to this volume, let us carry with us the lessons learned, the memories shared, and the laughter enjoyed. And let us look forward to the next chapter in our cricketing adventure, knowing that the spirit of cricket – with all its passion, its drama, and its sheer unpredictability – will continue to inspire us for generations to come.

So, until we meet again on the pitch, thank you for being a part of "Pitch Tales." May your love for the game burn bright, and may the stories we've shared bring a smile to your face whenever you need it most.

With warmest regards,
Divyanshu Gaur

www.ingramcontent.com/pod-product-compliance
Lightning Source LLC
Chambersburg PA
CBHW030238150726

47988CB00021B/3150